Christopher Wills

PROPERTY INVESTMENT

Appraisal and Valuation

Contents

    1.

    2.

    3.

    4.

    5.

    6.

    7.

1

Acknowledgments

Much thanks to you for your advantage in our property. We trust that we can furnish you with the data you're looking for on this property, yet kindly note that these are not restricting offers and are dependent upon future developments until an understanding has been reached between us. Any offers made by us will be likely to survey by our overseeing specialists who will go with the last choice on offers.

2

Who is property investment?

Property venture is large business, and, whenever done appropriately, can immediately turn out to be profoundly worthwhile. It includes the acquisition of a property, regularly one that is as yet being worked (off-plan property), with the end goal of improving it and either selling it on or renting it out to acquire a return. Property venture can likewise be directed on any scale, from basically buying one more home to building a business out of such speculations.

Many flourishing property venture organizations were shaped from responsibility for unit. When one property becomes two and two becomes four, the compounding phenomenon kicks in and with it a developing energy to buy and create a gain from property. Purchasing and possessing land is a venture procedure that can be both fulfilling and worthwhile. Dissimilar to stock and bond financial backers, forthcoming land proprietors can utilize influence to purchase a property by paying a piece of the complete expense forthright, then taking care of the equilibrium, in addition to intrigue, over the long haul.

However a conventional home loan for the most part requires a 20% to 25% initial installment, at times, a 5% initial installment is everything necessary to buy a whole property. This capacity to control the resource the second papers are marked encourages both land flippers and property managers, who can, thus, require out second home loans on their homes to make initial installments on extra properties. The following are five key ways financial backers can bring in cash on land.

Land is an unmistakable resource class that numerous specialists concur ought to be a piece of a very much differentiated portfolio. This is on the grounds that land doesn't generally intently associate with stocks, bonds, or items. Land speculations can likewise deliver pay from rents or home loan installments notwithstanding the potential for capital increases. Put resources into something beyond property so your cash isn't across the board market. In the event that you put resources into one market, it'll expand your gamble and means your portfolio isn't broadened. See pick your ventures for how to track down different speculations to assist you with arriving at your objectives.

The choice to purchase a speculation property ought to be important for your money growth strategy and think about your objectives and hazard resistance.

When you have a property at the top of the priority list, contrast the pay you expect with your active costs. In the event that there is a deficiency, consider whether you can cover the costs long haul. Likewise, resolve whether you could cover all costs present moment in the event that you had no occupants for some time.

Research the property market to choose how to get a speculation property. Where and what you purchase will influence your profit from speculation.

5 critical elements in property speculation achievement

Property stays a bedrock in solid speculation systems, as the market scene and the requirements of purchasers keeps on developing. Putting resources into new homes and land as opposed to existing properties offers a one of a kind scope of advantages, giving you pick shrewdly, plan completely and remain aware of dangers.

While there is no impenetrable venture equation (and anybody selling you one ought to be accepted tentatively), there are key elements illuminating speculation choices that - whenever considered and obliged - for the most part work on your possibilities going with decisions that convey benefits over the long run.

These five elements — timing, area, quality, hazard, cost and arrangement — are critical to comprehend and anticipate. We should take a gander at them corresponding to new homes and land.

- Timing

Assuming that you're purchasing a more seasoned, laid out property, you'll commonly simply be seeking the general market for signs to act. Is it a purchasers' market? Is a rural area overheated or on the ascent?

While you're putting resources into new homes, you additionally need to consider the planning of your up front investment to the undertaking. On the off chance that you secure your part and arrangement in the beginning phases of another turn of events, the degree for development is the best it will at any point be, and your speculation is essentially ensured future capital development. The later you normally pause, the lower your profits are probably going to be.

While it's actual there is at times less gamble purchasing later in an undertaking, the other side of decreased risk is lesser returns. To boost your development, search for open doors in the earliest potential phases of improvements from accomplices with a history you trust.

- Area

It's the most established land adage in the book (area, area, area), yet it's a fundamental thought while you're putting resources into new properties. You need extraordinary homes in high-development regions where request areas of strength for is.

Guarantee the improvement you're thinking about buying inside approaches current or arranged conveniences and is in solid closeness to development passages in the area. Search for government framework speculation and interest from private endeavor in working out the area.

For your speculation to flourish, you'll have to have stable tenures. Australian inhabitants' noise for properties that suit their everyday requirements and take care of the way of life they need to live. New improvements are frequently well known with youthful families, or occupants who need to partake in a more secure, more tranquil lifestyle, without forfeiting current comforts and admittance to metropolitan regions in the event that they need it.

Ensure your improvement is some place you're sure local people will need to reside, work and play.

- Quality

In the event that everything looks good and the area is awesome, yet the nature of the home item doesn't measure up, your venture may at last battle.

Land is valuable, however your future occupants (and purchasers) will need a property on that land they can be glad for. Guarantee the development specialists, planners and property administrators forming your speculation are qualified, experienced and can take care of business.

Go for the gold floor-plans, areas and determinations are financial backer streamlined, and where there are considerations accessible to drive esteem all through the whole speculation life-cycle by expanding rental pay, limit your upkeep costs and boosting future capital worth.

- Cost and arrangement

New homes and land are in many cases an opportunity to enter a sought after market at a cutthroat cost.

Recognize cost contributions that are serious with the middle house cost for the locale and no secret strings or additional items. Approve these against market measures. You maintain that your property should be turn-key for your inhabitants upon the arrival of settlement, not need additional work or cost from you before you can begin acquiring.

Search for bargains that permit you to follow up on the right timing, for instance, a little store and a cool off period that permits you to confirm your monetary limit and complete your reasonable level of investment without pressure. This allows you to take the smart actions while you set up your arrangements.

- Risk

No venture is without risk. However, working with the right accomplice and groups ought to ease irrational gamble and set out open doors for you.

Search out engineers and specialists that are ready to work with you to decrease chance to you and your venture, and instances of financial backers who have had achievement working with those specialists.

You ought to continuously feel open to asking your designer or specialist inquiries to more readily comprehend the gamble profile of the property being referred to, for example, what is the most extreme time a form could take, and do you have ensure for   surrenders?

3

Which investment property to buy

While properties near the city will generally see higher development than territorial properties, numerous financial backers are currently estimated out of city showcases however can in any case find great open doors further abroad. With respect to local regions, we have seen a few astounding open doors for clients over the most recent few years.

"A territorial region that performs well for the most part has consistent populace development, business open doors, way of life highlights, (for example, a tree-change, ocean change local area) and foundation improvement works, in addition to other things.

"This adds to an interest for lodging so financial backers can get another house and land bundle at a substantially more sensible cost than a ghetto property and can bring higher rental yields, which could see the speculation being income positive.

- House or unit?

Once more, there's a spot for the two houses and units in a property venture portfolio, contingent upon your conditions.

"Houses in developing regions will generally encounter higher capital development than units or condos because of the land content.

"The drawback of this is that the rental yields contrasted with the worth of the property are much of the time lower than that of a unit.

"Likewise, a house versus a unit in a similar area is for the most part going to be more costly, and that implies it will influence the financial backer's capacity to continue to get to gain further speculations.

- New or laid out?

Most exhortation around property buying shows more seasoned houses or units have better potential for capital development, and Christopher concurs, but he says it's an instance of good fits for each situation.

Laid out homes are by and large bound to have their own property, which can give colossal lifts in esteem. They likewise have better degree for discussion on cost, and further worth can be added through remodel, region or advancement.

Yet, Christopher says properties that are extremely old will keep you from guaranteeing numerous deterioration advantages, and will draw in lower rental yields and higher support costs.

New properties, then again, offer a lot higher deterioration and much lower stamp obligation whenever paid off-the-plan.

"Deterioration can be guaranteed at a lot higher rate than with a more seasoned property. This can assist with adjusting the incomes of a property and at times, making the property income positive.

- **Purchasing a house as a property speculation**

Houses will generally cost more to keep up with than condos, since proprietors are liable for the expense of fixes all around.

The potential gain of possessing a house according to a financial backer's point of view is that you can make upgrades to your property without endorsement from another party, like a proprietors' enterprise.

Benefits

* Houses can possibly fill in esteem

* Occupants pay higher lease to live in a property

* Alluring highlights for tenants, for example, patios, vehicle leaving and different rooms and restrooms

* Can have loads of degree to work on the worth and allure of the property through redesigns, increments and arranging

* Different parking spaces might be accessible

Drawbacks

* Houses are more costly than units

* Rental reimbursements may not cover month to month advance and different costs

- **LAND**

It's frequently been suggested that individuals ought to purchase land because of its shortage. Considering this, financial backers need to comprehend the common sense of possessing land and of maintaining a land-based undertaking. They likewise should know about the particular sorts of land-related speculation choices accessible through venture items, for example, trade exchanged reserves (Etas) and trade exchanged notes (Tens).

Kinds of Land Speculations

Freely well off individuals can buy land for individual use, amusement, and indeed, speculation. Sadly, a great many people don't fall into this class. This makes one wonder: Are land-proprietorship valuable open doors and undertakings fit for creating a satisfactory profit from speculation for little financial backers, while as yet managing the cost of them the delights and properties related with land possession? To respond to this inquiry, you should have the option to assess not many general classes of potential land ventures:

    * Private advancement land

    * Business advancement land

    * Column crop land

Private and Business Land Speculations

Private and business land improvement offers a practical entrance into venture in light of the fact that basically a limitless number of land improvement valuable open doors can be organized to meet a financial backer's capital and time limitations. For most little financial backers, land venture trust

(REIT) Etas are an ideal decision since they don't need direct administration, they are comprehensively enhanced by property type, they are geologically expanded, they can be bought or sold consistently, and they are extremely cheap. Some work in a kind of land, yet others, like the Vanguard REIT ETF (VNQ), give differentiated openness to modern, office, retail, medical services, public capacity, and private property improvements.

Sadly, these sorts of speculations refute the capacity of the landowner to appreciate utilizing the land. Accordingly, private and business land improvements are not doable choices for individuals that need to encounter the sensation of land proprietorship really.

Line Harvest Endlessly land for Domesticated animals Activities

Land bought for line crop cultivating or for running a domesticated animals activity bears the cost of the capacity to appreciate land in the home-owning sense, as well as from the viewpoint of creating pay. Notwithstanding, there are a large group of issues for little financial backers who buy land to work these sorts of undertakings. In the first place, the scale expected to work a column crop activity or animals activity must be exceptionally enormous to be monetarily feasible. This, thusly, requires a huge forthright capital cost a long ways past what a great many people can manage. Also, the continuous fixed costs related with running these sorts of cultivating activities are very high.

This, thus, implies that the monetary influence and business risk for such tasks are exceptionally high also. Subsequently, a lot of pressure is placed on the landowner to make these sorts of undertakings monetarily effective. By and large, the feeling of anxiety far surpasses the advantages that individuals long for as landowners. In light of this, it is a fair evaluation to say that most little financial backers ought to try not to seek after these sorts of enormous scope cultivating tasks, as the dangers and difficulties of such action will probably surpass any advantages.

While possessing a conventional column harvest or domesticated animals cultivating activity is likely not practical for most little financial backers, numerous rural speculation choices give satisfactory venture openness to customary cultivating undertakings. For instance, a few assets give openness to soybeans, corn, wheat, cotton, sugar, espresso, soybean oil, live steers, feeder cows, cocoa, lean swines, Kansas City wheat, canola oil, and soybean dinner. Consequently, by putting resources into this item, little financial backers will have expansive venture openness to customary cultivating activities. This, thus, can be utilized by the financial backer to help stay informed concerning conventional cultivating rehearses, as well as to produce an appealing profit from speculation over the long haul.

Little financial backers can likewise use an assortment of trade exchanged notes (ETNs) to put resources into explicit kinds of conventional cultivating tasks.

4

Where is good property investment

You can find speculation properties all over the place, in both modest communities and enormous urban areas. You could figure you can find speculation homes in princely areas. In any case, you can likewise find venture properties in areas that are exceptional. Assuming you purchase before that area becomes hot, you could grab a permanent spot for a minimal expense that will sell at a lot higher figure once you're prepared to sell.

You could try and find a speculation property in areas that are recorded as any open door zones. Financial backers get tax cuts whenever they sink their dollars into opportunity zones - regions that have been recognized as low-pay regions - to draw in new venture to neighborhoods frequently horribly needing it. Nobody housing market is ideal for each financial backer. A lot of what makes a city the ideal put for your speculation dollars relies upon your drawn out objectives.

Might it be said that you are keen on gathering month to month lease checks? Then, at that point, a famous vacationer location may be best for you. Is it true that you are more worried about watching your speculation property expansion in esteem after some time? Then, at that point, a significant city with a developing populace and rising property estimations may be the better decision. Is it true that you are restricted on reserves? You could pick a local that you think will fill in prominence soon yet includes more cheap homes today.

Beside the property's area, it's likewise vital to take a gander at a couple of other key variables while assessing rental returns and picking where to contribute. For instance, you ought to know about the area's lease as a level of pay, opportunity rate, home costs, industry, populace and development rate.

1. Houston, Texas

Known for space investigation, the requirement for a lot of cooling, worldwide energy and oil investigation, also being home to more than 2.3 million individuals, the Houston region has a ton making it work. Notwithstanding its financial assets, Houston is notable for its reasonable lodging. The middle deals cost of a current home in Houston hit $324,881 in Spring of 2022, up 11.2% from 1 year sooner.

Its home costs, joined with its clamoring business scene, make Houston an undeniable area for land financial backers. It's likewise a decent market for rental pay. Single-family home rentals rose 7.1% in 2021, while the typical month to month lease expanded 8.5% to $2,042. Apartment and condo leases expanded 5.1% with the typical month to month lease up 3.8% to $1,737 - all uplifting news for land financial backers.

2. Charlotte, North Carolina

A city with a populace of more than 874,000 as per the 2020 enumeration, Charlotte, nicknamed the "Sovereign City," positions among the best urban communities in the US for organizations and vocations. Charlotte is home to in excess of 10 Fortune 1000 organizations, including Bank of America, Lowe's and Wachovia Corp., and highlights various foundations of higher learning, social focuses and medical care offices.

The middle deals cost of a current home in Charlotte remained at $350,019 in Spring of 2022. That is up 18.8% and $55,451 from that very month 1j year sooner. This makes Charlotte one of the most smoking land areas in the US. The typical lease for a one-room condo in Charlotte in late April was $1,433, a 19% increment contrasted with last year's measurements, as per Zumper.

3. Orlando, Florida

Orlando's radiant scenes mean a lot of chances for land financial backers across its more prominent metropolitan region. This may be the top vacationer city in the US. In any case, the Orlando region likewise lives it up populace of more than 2.03 million individuals, an increment of 1.8% from a year sooner. The city is supposed to bring down the 2.9 million occupant mark in 2025.

Orlando is likewise known for work development, especially in its travel industry and relaxation and neighborliness ventures. Florida's absence of state personal expense and warm weather conditions energizes a great many individuals and organizations to change areas from other metropolitan regions that aren't so charge indulgent and where the cost for many everyday items is higher.

The middle deals cost of a current home in Orlando was $296,193 in Spring of 2022, up 10% from that very month in 2021.The normal lease for a one-room condo in Orlando was $1,679 in late April, a 35% expansion contrasted with a similar time last year, as per Zumper.

4. Portland, Maine

At the point when you consider Maine, you could picture rough drifts, beacons and lobster. Be that as it may, you should contemplate speculation properties, as well. Land venture could seem OK in the smallish yet curious town of Portland, Maine.

With in excess of 66,000 occupants, you'll track down imaginative food, a thriving horticulture industry and oceans of sea history in Portland, Maine. It's likewise a well known landing objective for home purchasers and planned purchasers searching for a more open optional city. This implies that this city is likewise a decent hotspot for month to month rental pay.

In Spring of 2022, home costs in Portland, Maine, expanded 19.9% contrasted with last year, with homes here selling at a middle cost of $523,000. Homes in Portland were likewise selling in 6 days on normal in Walk, a major drop from the 41 days on normal it took for homes to sell here last Walk. Likewise as of Spring of 2022, the normal lease for a loft in Portland was $1,607, as per information from Rent Cafe.

5. Atlanta, Georgia

With its populace approaching a portion of 1,000,000 as of the 2020 registration, Atlanta is one of the more quickly developing urban communities in the Unified State. This Georgia city is known for its rich history, imaginative personalities it's one of two urban communities on the planet to enjoy housed two Nobel Harmony Prize champs - and numerous vacation destinations.

Atlanta's populace development, and the interest for homes in this market, pursue this city a decent decision for financial backers, whether they are depending on month to month lease or keen on clutching a property while its worth increments.

The middle sold cost for an Atlanta home rose to $374,249 in Spring, up 13.6% from a year sooner. How solid is interest for lodging here? Of the 1,146 homes sold in Spring of 2022, a great 504 were sold over asking cost. As per Zumper, the typical month to month lease for a one-room condo in Atlanta was $1,700 as mid-April of this current year. That is up 16% from a year sooner.

6. Phoenix, Arizona

With more than 1.6 million occupants, the suitably nicknamed "Valley of the Sun," also called Phoenix, Arizona, offers all year warmth, lovely vistas, verifiable sights, a lot of diversion and nightlife and a developing number of business valuable open doors. As additional individuals look to move to this warm-climate city, both Phoenix's lodging values and condo rents have been developing quickly.

The numbers recount the tale of an especially hot real estate market in Phoenix: In Spring, the middle deals cost of a Phoenix home was $400,005, a strong increment of 25% from that very month in 2021. Purchasers are getting these homes rapidly, with 2,300 selling in Walk, a leap of 18.7%. Purchasers frequently address more than posting cost here, with 59% of homes selling for more than whatever their dealers requested in Spring.

The typical month to month lease for a condo in Phoenix was $1,547 in Spring, as per Rent Cafe.

7. Salt Lake City, Utah

Salt Lake City's rich strict culture, authentic destinations and normal milestones - particularly that broadly pungent lake and the mountains encompassing the city - can't be overlooked. They draw the two vacationers and new occupants to this cut of the country. There are a ton of advantages to putting resources into the Salt Lake City housing market, including Utah's vertical moving position development, low joblessness rate and low state and neighborhood charges.

Salt Lake City additionally offers high inhabitant rates, and that intends that since investment properties are sought after, occupants might be more able to remain in your investment property as long as possible.

Salt Lake City positioned among the best five of 51 metropolitan regions in the US this February as far as deals cost development, as per a RE/MAX report. The organization's public lodging report for February said that Salt Lake City homes sold at a middle cost of $516,759 that month. That is a leap of 26% from the middle cost of $410,000 in February of 2021.

inhabitant revealed in late April that the middle month to month loft lease for Salt Lake City was a strong $1,562.

8. Minneapolis-St. Paul, Minnesota

On the off chance that you knew about the Midwest, you definitely realize that the locale is dabbed with generally modest single-family rental homes and little multifamily structures, which makes this piece of the country a shrewd decision for land financial backers. What's more, the Twin Urban communities of Minneapolis and St. Paul are a genuine illustration of what Midwest markets bring to the table for financial backers.

The Twin Urban communities region brags bounty reasonable lodging choices, yet in addition offers culture, a clamoring food scene, pro athletics and a lot of Fortune 500 organizations.

The Twin Urban communities region, with multiple million occupants in the urban areas themselves and their rural areas, is one of the most populated metro regions in the Midwest and one of the more reasonable spots in which to live. That means generally speaking less expensive land buy and holding costs for you. The region likewise offers high business rates, occupations in various enterprises, magnificent colleges and schools and an interest for rental lodging.

The middle deals cost of homes sold in Minneapolis in Spring hit $318,165, an increment of 4% from a year sooner. In St. Paul, that number was $265,609, a leap of 10% from a year sooner. The typical lease for a one-room condo in St. Paul in April was $1,110, as per Zumper, a leap of 6% when contrasted with the earlier year. In Minneapolis, that figure was $1,175, a decline of 3% from a year sooner.

9. Indianapolis, Indiana

While Indianapolis is most popular for the celebrated Indianapolis 500, the world's biggest single-day game, the Indiana city brings more to the table than this renowned auto race. There are major-association sports establishments, exceptionally positioned exhibition halls, colleges, shops, eateries and family-accommodating exercises for those with small kids.

The Indianapolis real estate market draws in many out-of-state financial backers due to its low lodging costs contrasted with numerous different regions in the nation, similar to the east and west drifts. These lower costs imply that financial backers needn't bother with their properties to appreciate however much they do in greater expense markets.

The ongoing middle deals cost of homes in Indianapolis was $216,964 in Spring of this current year, an increment of 17.3% from that very month a year prior. The typical month to month condo lease for Indianapolis was $1,055 in February.

10. Birmingham, Alabama

The second-biggest city in Alabama probably won't strike a chord when you initially think about purchasing land in the profound South. Be that as it may, Birmingham's reasonable lodging and minimal expense of living can make putting resources into land a less exorbitant recommendation. What's more, lodging costs here are on the ascent.

In Spring of 2022, the middle deals cost of homes in Birmingham came in at $197,000. That is reasonable. Simultaneously, home estimations here have been ascending, with Spring's figure up 16.3% when contrasted with that very month a year sooner. This implies that financial backers don't need to concoct as much cash forthright while purchasing land here yet can in any case sensibly anticipate that the worth of their buys should increment. Keep in mind, however, as in all business sectors, this isn't ensured.

Youthful experts and families find that Birmingham has an incredible work market, especially for medical care, assembling and government business. Weighing in at in excess of 330,000 occupants, as per the U.S. Statistics Department's 2020 numbers, Birmingham offers more going on under the surface.

Zumper reports that the typical lease for a one-room loft in Birmingham remained at $1,000 in April. That is a leap of 11% when contrasted with that very month a year sooner.

Urban communities with solid real estate markets and venture potential are spread the nation over, and there are a lot of extra business sectors excluded from this rundown that would likewise make a decent home for your land speculation dollars.

5

Are investment property depreciated

One of the biggest tax cuts for proprietors of speculation property comes as devaluation, or the misfortune in worth of a property after some time because of actual crumbling. The U.S. Interior Income Administration (IRS) permits proprietors to assume an expense misfortune consistently founded on this devaluation over the helpful existence of the resource, known as the expense recuperation period. This choice can lessen their available pay by huge number of dollars every year.

The plot of land on which the structure rests, in any case, isn't dependent upon devaluation since it is named a non-depreciable resource, or one that can't lose esteem. This really intends that assuming an assessor esteems your all out property at $300,000 and the land on which it sits is esteemed at $25,000, the property's appreciable worth beginnings at $275,000. The property can be degraded at a consistent rate for an endorsed time frame , which, starting around 2011, is 27½ years for homes and 39 years for business properties. In a similar model, the property will deteriorate at $10,000 each year until it has no worth (on paper) 27½ years after the fact. Regardless of whether the home's surveyed esteem has significantly increased during that time span, it is viewed as useless to the IRS.

The catch, tragically, is that the deterioration sums that you discount will diminish your unique speculation for the property, called the changed premise, accordingly expanding the available benefit you should pronounce when you sell the property. For example, on the off chance that the proprietor of a property bought for $250,000 took $200,000 in derivations when it was sold for $225,000, the proprietor would need to pay charges on a $175,000 benefit despite the fact that he wrote off his venture. The IRS doesn't offer a "free lunch"; deterioration just permits a speculation land owner to pay for his feast long after he's eaten it.

Tips and Alerts for Proprietors of Speculation Properties

* Proprietors ought to continuously guarantee the right measure of deterioration each fiscal year on the grounds that the IRS will expect it was taken. As a result, your changed premise in the property will be diminished as per the tax break you ought to have taken, regardless of whether you take it. Unclaimed deterioration might be represented in future assessment forms, with specific impediments.

* Speculation property doesn't start deteriorating upon its buy or when the occupants really take inhabitant except if these dates agree with the date that the property is rental-prepared. For example, assume you buy a property in April and make enhancements until June, when you start publicizing it as a

rental, yet you can't sign occupants until August. As per the IRS, the devaluation time frame starts in June.

* Shutting costs, for example, review and evaluation charges, as well as different costs related with the first acquisition of the house, combine with your changed premise in the property. Costs caused after the property has been leased, like remodels and significant upgrades, are typically deteriorated independently from the remainder of the property's price tag.

* In spite of the fact that you can't devalue land, you can deteriorate arranging and other land readiness costs brought about while setting up the land for business use.

* Your deterioration allowance for the main year depends on the mid-month show, in which you can deduct just 50% of the primary month's devaluation. Assuming you start leasing a property on July third, you can deduct 5½ long periods of devaluation for the main year - not the full a half year that the rental was working.

* Check with the IRS to ensure that your property qualifies as depreciable property, as private homes that are utilized for under half business purposes may not qualify. IRS rules additionally make sense of different things that might be discounted as depreciable misfortunes, from normal office gear to intriguing creatures.

* Employ a certified proficient to survey the worth of the property before its buy. The IRS requires an itemized assessor's gauge of the property's estimation before you can start guaranteeing deterioration misfortunes on your expense form.

* Continuously recruit an InterNACHI auditor to inspect a speculation property for abandons before it is bought. Assume the review uncovers that one of the rooms in a three-room condo is non-adjusting; you'll be aware ahead of the buy that you can't legitimately depend on 33% of your expected rental pay without critical and exorbitant changes. InterNACHI auditors are likewise prepared to uncover a grouping of security and framework absconds, from bug invasion to the presence of toxic paint and shape.

Besides, Speculation property deterioration is a legitimate expense derivation connected with the mileage of your venture property. Set forth plainly, you might have the option to guarantee an expense derivation because of your property progressing in years with time. The sum you can guarantee will differ in light of the particular property you have bought and when it was fabricated. The underneath figures are gauges in view of the normal of genuine reports we've finished at Washington Brown.

In the event that you purchase a property worked between the years 1987 and 2000, you might have the option to guarantee generally $4,000 in derivations a year, or near $40,000 over the initial 10 years.

In the event that you purchase a property worked between the years 2000 and 2020, it's probably you'll have the option to guarantee around $6,500 per year, or near $65,000 over the initial 10 years you own the property.

In the event that you purchase a spic and span property, you might be qualified for guarantee roughly $16,000 in year one and near $100,000 over the initial 10 years.

If it's not too much trouble, note, in any case, that these figures are planned as a guideline gauge as opposed to a conclusive estimation of the amount you'll have the option to guarantee in devaluation.

The subject of deterioration on land speculations and its effect on charges stood out as truly newsworthy after President Trump expressed that devaluation was the justification behind the $1 billion in misfortunes he endured before he was chosen — misfortunes that permitted him to try not to pay charges for a long time.

Benefits from deterioration can affect land financial backers' expenses in critical ways, saving them hundreds to thousands of dollars each year. Land deterioration is characterized as a personal duty derivation that permits a citizen to recuperate the expense (or other premise) of a land venture. The deterioration is acknowledged as a sort of derivation that diminishes the financial backer's available pay.

In contrast to rental costs — which incorporate things like fix and support costs, venture out costs connected with property the executives, work space costs, local charges, contract protection, property protection, and expert administrations — that can be deducted from rental pay brought in the year the cash was spent, devaluation deducts the expense of purchasing and working on an investment property over the helpful existence of the property.

While deterioration seems like a definite bet for decreasing land financial backers' charges, it is vital to take note of that the IRS has extremely nitty gritty and complex guidelines about how devaluation can be utilized as an expense derivation. Devaluation is the misfortune in worth to a structure over the long run because old enough, mileage, and disintegration. You can likewise incorporate land upgrades you've made and things inside the property that are not piece of the structure like apparatus and covering.

Basically, investment property deterioration permits financial backers discount the construction and upgrades to the property throughout some stretch of time. This is an "cost" that you can use as a discount on your expenses.

Nonetheless, you can deteriorate the upgrades to the actual construction - not the land..

Each financial backer has an "Venture Property Procedure", expanding how much return you get on your speculation property at charge time is an essential component to be remembered for that system. While devaluation tax reductions are predominately more prominent on fresher properties, they are material for all speculation properties and ought to be integrated into your Methodology regardless of a property's development date and development type. The most common way of asserting deterioration straightforwardly works on your income by diminishing your available pay or assessable pay, and in like manner, builds the possibility to grow your portfolio further.

6

Where to sell your investment property

Pursuing the choice to sell your venture property is invigorating and enabling — particularly taking into account the exhibition of the ongoing business sector. You're perched on a high-esteem property and every one of the long stretches of work to create your financial well being is going to pay off. Whether you need to reinvest that cash somewhere else, use it to support travel around. To do this, it's fundamental you have all the vital data to without hesitation travel through this. Selling your property venture is no joking matter. You really want to conclude whether you need to go through the problem of tracking down a purchaser, figuring out it with your landowner, and afterward moving out of the property or whether you maintain that should do it all yourself. To do it all yourself, then you'll have to realize about tax reductions for trading investment properties. This will give you some cash back in what you pay in lease every year. You'll likewise have the option to guarantee costs connected with selling your home including legitimate expenses and promoting costs along with contract interest on any advances utilized while trading the actual property.

In the event that you figure this may be excessively convoluted for you, there are expert organizations who can assist with this cycle for an expense; these may incorporate home specialists who can assist with finding possible purchasers for your property and conveyances who can deal with all legitimate prerequisites associated with selling the actual property. Selling your property venture is an interesting business. Here are a few hints to make the cycle more straightforward:

-Ensure you have sufficient opportunity to sell your property. Be ready for a long deals interaction and give yourself sufficient opportunity to do everything before you really want to continue on.

-On the off chance that you are not selling on time, consider recruiting a specialist or representative who will assist you with selling your property. They can deal with the subtleties, like promoting and showcasing, as well as handle desk work and legitimate parts of the deal. At the point when you initially choose to sell your property, be certain that anything cost you set for it is sensible in view of its condition and area. You need to receive however much cash as could reasonably be expected in return while as yet saving a sound profit from venture for yourself!

The principal thing to do when you need to sell your property venture is to track down a purchaser. You can do this by publicizing in papers, on the web, or even via virtual entertainment. Mainly, you make it happen as fast as could be expected, ideally inside the primary month of posting your property available to be purchased.

Whenever you have tracked down a purchaser, then now is the ideal time to begin arranging terms. This stage can be somewhat precarious on the grounds that it includes the two players concocting an arrangement over what they figure the property ought to be worth and the amount they will pay for it. You want to fulfill sure that the two players are with what they have settled upon prior to marking anything and not just in light of the fact that you would rather not wind up paying more than you ought to be paying yet additionally in light of the fact that this could influence your capacity to sell the property in later years assuming things turn out badly!

Whenever everything is settled upon and approved by the two players then you really want to plan administrative work, for example, an agreement of offer which will detail all parts of how things work between yourselves (the vender) and yourself (the purchaser). It likewise incorporates data about who possesses what on the property - who pays charge on it and so on.

Selling a house: The timing, process and cost

While properties are sold all year, a few seasons are more rewarding for selling. Truth be told, the pandemic changed this and the housing market has been hot from that point onward. In this way, you don't have to stress over timing, as we're in an economically difficult market. There are a lot of explanations behind selling speculation property — for retirement, on the off chance that it's not performing great, to re-contribute, to get to Capital Increases Expense exclusion, or essentially on the grounds that now is the right time. Carve out opportunity to think about these focuses, tending to both the intelligent and close to home reasons. You'll know when it feels right.

To work on the cycle, there's five moves toward take to sell your speculation property.

* Figure out how much your property is worth

* Contrast reactors with track down the best met for your requirements

* Think about your assessment repercussions

* Pick whether it's ideal to sell by means of closeout or secretly

* Ensure your representative and occupants are in correspondence. Get the help to help you through the excursion (favoring this later).

Since you're selling a property that is likewise somebody's home, set aside some margin to look for a way to improve on the tenure understanding and the regulations in your state. Be adaptable with the requirements of your inhabitants, as they should leave sooner in the event that they track down another spot to live.

It's likewise beneficial to begin assembling a rundown of things you really want to do before you put the property available. Whenever you've informed the inhabitants, deal with any underlying fixes and clean the house available to be purchased. Search for chances to build the asking cost.

While each house is unique, remember these normal expenses related with selling a venture property:

* The specialist's bonus

* Showcasing and promoting costs

* Conveyancing charges

* Conclusion of home loan and advance breaking costs (assuming that you have one)

* Property show and styling

* Capital additions charge

* Disengaging utilities.

Capital increases on houses

Selling your speculation property is a significant monetary and way of life choice. You most likely have many inquiries, for example, what assessment do I pay? What costs could I at any point guarantee? Shouldn't something be said about Capital Increases Expense (CGT)? How might I compute charge gain or misfortune on an offer of an investment property?

Indeed, since your property isn't your fundamental home, there's a duty on selling a house — Capital Increases Expense (CGT). Venture properties and occasion property holders are expected to pay this duty after selling. The duty rate relies upon your available pay in the time of the deal. You're qualified for a half markdown (on the off chance that you've possessed the property for over a year).

There are three different ways for working out your Capital Increases Duty on a land property: the rebate technique, the indexation strategy, year possession period strategy. By taking care of business with research charge on land gains, you'll have the option to diminish the amount you pay (or even keep away from it out and out).

A portion of the choices are to utilize the transitory nonattendance rule, put resources into superannuation, and getting the planning of your capital increase or misfortune right. For instance, assuming that you anticipate your pay in the following monetary year, you can defer selling, so your lower minor duty rate implies you'll pay less CGT.

7

Can property investment make you rich

here is no speedy method for making cash or get wealthy in land, yet you can create financial well being gradually and consistently by making wise speculations. You're presumably mindful that there are various ways to abundance. Nonetheless, one of the huge ways of gathering abundance is through land. Making abundance through land, then again, requires sound counsel, frameworks, and steadiness.

Land financial planning is a dependable method for bringing in cash, yet it accompanies gambles, very much like some other business. Land can be a fantastic way to gather abundance whenever done accurately. This is valid assuming that you require some investment to find out about the interaction and the best ways of amplifying your benefits.

It's a lot simpler to start land putting away on the off chance that you have cash (basically a 20% initial investment). Be that as it may, numerous business people start their organizations with very little cash, including land effective money management.

A considerable lot of them succeed basically by thinking beyond practical boundaries and investing some parcel of energy. Accordingly, we composed this article for those new to the land who needs to figure out how to bring in cash. Land can possibly make you affluent. There are different land speculation choices accessible today; there is nobody size-fits-all arrangement. Figuring out how to bring in cash in land is one of the best ways of differentiating your portfolio. You could purchase an underestimated land property, fix it up, and offer it to a financial backer assuming that you have a lot of cash. After the work gets finished, you benefit by selling the property at a lot greater expense than you paid for it. You could likewise purchase an excursion property or a drawn out investment property.

You can lease it out to others when it's not getting utilized. On the off chance that you'd rather use your venture by buying an occupant prepared property with a home loan, this is valid. You can create financial stability, safeguard against expansion, and benefit from a rising business sector by making the legitimate strides. Influence, appreciation, and tax cuts are only a couple of the advantages of possessing land. Getting a decent arrangement can be a fantastic long haul speculation too. Adding a land portfolio can assist with broadening your possessions. This segment will zero in on different techniques for becoming well off in land. Do you have any assumptions? Land can work in more ways than one to assist you with developing your riches. We should get everything rolling and perceive how you can be a fruitful land financial backer.

Investment properties as a type of revenue in land

This is the customary strategy for amassing abundance in land. Long haul purchase and-hold private rentals become acclimated to bringing in cash in this sort of speculation.

A spot to live will constantly get required. Masters and aristocrats battled about titles that permitted them to gather lease from the people who lived, cultivated, or dealt with their property in another way.

A couple of venturesome people emptied out wastelands and laid out organizations to benefit more starting from the earliest stage in the event that they had rented it to ranchers and farmers.

We've made considerable progress in the meantime, giving a large number of choices for those keen on figuring out how to bring in cash in land. You could buy land, build a house, and lease it out. You could search for troubled properties, recovery them, and afterward exchange them.

This is the customary technique for collecting abundance in land. Long haul purchase and-hold private rentals become acclimated to bringing in cash in this kind of venture.

A spot to live will constantly get required. Masters and aristocrats battled about titles that permitted them to gather lease from the people who lived, cultivated, or dealt with their property in another way.

A couple of venturesome people emptied out wastelands and laid out organizations to benefit more starting from the earliest stage in the event that they had rented it to ranchers and farmers.

We've made considerable progress meanwhile, giving a large number of choices for those keen on figuring out how to bring in cash in land. You could buy land, build a house, and lease it out. You could search for troubled properties, recovery them, and afterward exchange them. Land can get bought for private, business, or modern use. The consistent income created by rental land is one of the main benefits of claiming it.

It's the best method for procuring an automated revenue from venture land. The weakness of this technique is that it thinks each of your eggs in few crates. The rental pay endures on the off chance that you own a high rise as inhabitants leave, or fix costs eat your benefits.

Then again, when you have various investment properties, this procedure is presumably the probably going to permit you to produce a reliable pay sufficiently huge to live on.

Putting resources into contract notes gives interest-just pay

Contract notes can be a decent choice for a recurring source of income. You get regularly scheduled installments that incorporate interest and head when you purchase a home loan note. It's a standard kind of revenue, like what you'd get from a rental.

In any case, there is compelling reason need to keep the property in respectable shape like a landowner would. Selecting land the nation over is undeniably more helpful on the grounds that you will not need to manage nearby land authorizing or charge guidelines.

The credit length gets expressed in the home loan note. You realize how long you'll need to take care of the advance, which could be somewhere in the range of 10 to 30 years.

By buying a home loan note from a troubled note holder, you might have the option to build the worth of the note. You could go over a ranch or a family home sold with proprietor supporting. One choice is a casual private land choice, which expects that you pay an expense, or premium, to reserve the option to purchase a house for a predefined period for a settled upon cost. You then find financial backers who will address more than your choice cost for the property. For this situation, the exceptional you get is basically a locator's expense for coordinating an individual searching for a speculation with an individual hoping to sell — the same than a Realtor's bonus, truly. Albeit this is pay, it doesn't come from purchasing (for example holding the deed to) a piece of land.

One choice is a casual private land choice, which expects that you pay an expense, or premium, to reserve the privilege to purchase a house for a predefined period for a settled upon cost. You then find financial backers who will follow through on more than your choice cost for the property. For this situation, the exceptional you get is basically a locator's charge for coordinating an individual searching for a venture with an individual hoping to sell — the same than a Realtor's bonus, truly. Albeit this is pay, it doesn't come from buying (for example holding the deed to) a piece of land.

Different choices include:

* Short deals — this includes buying a home from a bank when the mortgagee is behind on installments. Short deals can be a tedious and convoluted recommendation.

* Rent choices — these are what the name infers. At the point when you rent with a choice to purchase in a bull housing market, where costs are rising, you might have the option to finish the buy later at a lower, per-set cost, or create a gain by selling your buy freedoms.

* Contract flipping — rather than flipping houses, this sort of flipping includes the exchange of the freedoms of a buy agreement to another purchaser. In the event that you can find bothered merchants and propelled purchasers and unite them, you might have the option to create a gain along these lines.

The Reality

There are a few demonstrated techniques for bringing in cash in land. Appreciation, expansion, and pay rank high on the rundown yet a few elective land ventures likewise exist. Figuring out your ventures, dangers, and regardless of whether the general interaction is worth the effort depends on you.

8

Conclusion

All in all, we have observed that interest in property is a worthwhile and remunerating venture. Property has a background marked by being perhaps of the most steady speculation, with a yearly return of 10% or more. It additionally can possibly increment in esteem after some time, something that different speculations basically can't do. This should be visible as an incredible method for laying out a practical kind of revenue for yourself or your loved ones.